The Last Flapper

A One-Woman Play

by William Luce

Based on the writings of
Mrs. F. Scott Fitzgerald

A SAMUEL FRENCH ACTING EDITION

SAMUEL FRENCH

FOUNDED 1830

New York Hollywood London Toronto

SAMUELFRENCH.COM

Copyright © 1979, 1985, 1988, 1990 by William Luce

ALL RIGHTS RESERVED

CAUTION: Professionals and amateurs are hereby warned that *THE LAST FLAPPER* is subject to a Licensing Fee. It is fully protected under the copyright laws of the United States of America, the British Commonwealth, including Canada, and all other countries of the Copyright Union. All rights, including professional, amateur, motion picture, recitation, lecturing, public reading, radio broadcasting, television and the rights of translation into foreign languages are strictly reserved. In its present form the play is dedicated to the reading public only.

The amateur live stage performance rights to *THE LAST FLAPPER* are controlled exclusively by Samuel French, Inc., and licensing arrangements and performance licenses must be secured well in advance of presentation. PLEASE NOTE that amateur Licensing Fees are set upon application in accordance with your producing circumstances. When applying for a licensing quotation and a performance license please give us the number of performances intended, dates of production, your seating capacity and admission fee. Licensing Fees are payable one week before the opening performance of the play to Samuel French, Inc., at 45 W. 25th Street, New York, NY 10010.

Licensing Fee of the required amount must be paid whether the play is presented for charity or gain and whether or not admission is charged.

Stock licensing fees quoted upon application to Samuel French, Inc.

For all other rights than those stipulated above, apply to: William Morris Endeavor Entertainment, 1325 Avenue of the Americas, New York, NY 10019.

Particular emphasis is laid on the question of amateur or professional readings, permission and terms for which must be secured in writing from Samuel French, Inc.

Copying from this book in whole or in part is strictly forbidden by law, and the right of performance is not transferable.

Whenever the play is produced the following notice must appear on all programs, printing and advertising for the play: "Produced by special arrangement with Samuel French, Inc."

Due authorship credit must be given on all programs, printing and advertising for the play.

ISBN   978-0-573-69168-3   Printed   in   U.S.A.   #28001

To RAY

IMPORTANT BILLING AND CREDIT
REQUIREMENTS

All producers of *THE LAST FLAPPER must* give credit to
the Author and to Mrs. F. Scott Fitzgerald, in all programs
distributed in connection with performances of the Play and
in all instances in which the title of the Play appears for
purposes of advertising, publicizing or otherwise exploiting
the Play and/or a production. The name of the Author and
Mrs. F. Scott Fitzgerald *must* also appear on a separate
line, on which no other name appears, immediately
following the title, and *must* appear in size of type not less
than fifty percent the size of the title type. Said billing
must appear substantially as follows:

BY
WILLIAM LUCE
BASED ON THE WRITINGS OF
MRS. F. SCOTT FITZGERALD

No one shall commit or authorize any act or omission by which
the copyright of, or the right to copyright, this play may be
impaired.

No one shall make any changes in this play for the purpose of
production.

Publication of this play does not imply availability for
performance. Both amateurs and professionals considering a
production are *strongly* advised in their own interests to apply to
Samuel French, Inc., for written permission before starting
rehearsals, advertising, or booking a theatre.

No part of this book may be reproduced, stored in a retrieval
system, or transmitted in any form, by any means, now known
or yet to be invented, including mechanical, electronic,
photocopying, recording, videotaping, or otherwise, without the
prior written permission of the publisher.

THE NEUHAUS ARENA STAGE
SEPTEMBER 17 - OCTOBER 4, 1987

ALLEY THEATRE
Pat Brown, *Artistic/Executive Director*

presents

Piper Laurie

starring as 'Zelda' in

"THE LAST FLAPPER..

by William Luce

Based upon the writings of Mrs. F. Scott Fitzgerald.

Directed by

Charles Nelson Reilly

Costume Design
NOEL TAYLOR

Sound Design
TIMOTHY JOHN HELGESON

Set and Lighting Design
PATRICK HUGHES and CHRISTOPHER MANDICH

This production is made possible in part
by the Dudley and Tina Sharp New Plays Production Fund of the Alley Theatre Endowment

This production is underwritten by **ENRON CORP**

The Alley soars with ●CONTINENTAL AIRLINES

Actors and stage managers at Alley Theatre are members of Actors' Equity Association, the union for professionals in the legitimate theater. All members of the Alley's Sharp Young Company are Equity Membership Candidates. Alley directors are members of the Society of Stage Directors and Choreographers, the union for professional directors.

Alley Theatre is a constituent of Theatre Communications Group, the national service organization for non profit theaters, the American Arts Alliance, Texas Arts Alliance and the League of Resident Theatres. Seasonal operating expenses are partially supported by grants from the National Endowment for the Arts, the Texas Commission on the Arts, the Business Arts Fund, and by the Cultural Arts Council of Houston. Accommodations for many guest artists have been provided courtesy of the Four Seasons Place Apartments.

With few exceptions, costumes, scenery, and props used in Alley Theatre productions are constructed in the Alley's own backstage shops.

The photographing or sound recording of any performance or the possession of any device for such photographing or sound recording inside this theatre without the written permission of the management is prohibited by law. Violations may be punishable by ejection and may render the offender liable for monetary damages. Please refrain from the use of flashlights during the performance. Devices utilizing electronic sound alarms should be checked with the house manager.

· THE PRODUCTION ·

— CAST —

Zelda . . . PIPER LAURIE

Musical Design and Pianist: **Stan Freeman**
Choreographer: **Robert Fitch**
Stage Manager: **Mark Tynan**

— SCENES —

THE TIME:

Three o'clock p.m., March 10, 1948. Later that evening.
Zelda Fitzgerald perished in a fire at Highland Hospital

THE PLACE:

The office of Zelda's psychiatrist, Robert S. Carroll, M.D.
Highland Hospital, Asheville, North Carolina.

— There will be one intermission —

ACKNOWLEDGEMENTS

Exclusive tour direction: Kolmar-Luth Entertainment, Inc.
1501 Broadway, Suite 201
New York, NY 10036-5594
(212) 730-9500

Miss Laurie's costume is a copy of an original dress of Zelda Fitzgerald's
executed by Frank Bennett, Gilbert's of Hollywood
Piper Laurie and Charles Nelson Reilly would like to thank production associate
Sherrye Wade Cimino for her artful contribution to the fulfillment of the play.
Miss Laurie and Mr. Reilly would also like to thank Mr. James Albright.
Stardust Studios, Hollywood, CA
Program cover photograph: Zelda Fitzgerald, 1921
Program cover design by Carl Davis
Typesetting by The Art Table, Inc.

PREFACE

The evolution of a stage play is sometimes the work of years. Successive productions are an advantage to the playwright. He can observe and learn, alter and revise. And if he is fortunate enough to have an understanding, long-suffering publisher, he can even get his play reprinted.

The Last Flapper is such a play. As a revised dramatic work, it tried out at the Burt Reynold's Theatre in Jupiter, Florida in 1987. The play formally opened at the Alley Theatre in Houston, Texas, in September, 1987, and starred actress Piper Laurie, with direction by Charles Nelson Reilly. Originally titled *Zelda* and produced at off-Broadway's American Place Theatre, the earlier version starred actress Olga Bellin and was directed by Paul Roebling.

The Last Flapper is about the life of Zelda Fitzgerald, wife of novelist F. Scott Fitzgerald. My research into Zelda Fitzgerald's correspondence and other writings, published and unpublished, revealed to me a woman altogether different from the sentimental stereotype of the Fitzgerald legend.

Certainly, the legend is not the person. In *The Beautiful and the Damned,* Scott created Zelda a symbol of The Jazz Age — the Compleat Flapper, glamorous, vapid, selfish. Obligingly, Zelda played the role, for she was indeed daring, eccentric and passionate. But when the bad times came, and the wild, crazy escapades seemed sadly out of style, Zelda abandoned the legend.

Almost simultaneously, she entered the first of several mental hospitals wherein she would spend the rest of her life. Zelda's struggle for identification apart from Scott found expression in an autobiographical novel, *Save Me the Waltz*. Impressionistic in style, opulent in imagery, her writing is striking, powerful and undisciplined. Her published writings also include ten short stories.

Zelda was possessed of a brilliant, schizophrenic mind. She was exciting, original, witty, talented, tormented. All the ingredients for the stage. And her life was not all tragedy. That is the public cliché, the legend, not the reality. Zelda found self-completeness in her final years. Even though she was confined to institutions, her dignity held, and there was a kind of heroism in her. No self-pity, no wistful yearning for lost Utopias. I like that about Zelda. She was a lady with pride and guts.

Born in Montgomery, Alabama, on July 24, 1900, Zelda was 47 at the time of her tragic death. She was, in her own words, a "graduate of half a dozen mental institutes." She died in a fire at a sanitarium in Asheville, North Carolina, on March 10, 1948.

I would like to express my thanks not only to Scottie Fitzgerald Smith for permission to draw upon her mother's writings, but also to Professor

Matthew J. Bruccoli, Peter Shepherd of Harold Ober Associates, Gilbert Parker and Jerome Talbert of William Morris Agency, Paul and Olga Roebling, Abbott Van Nostrand of Samuel French, Inc., Piper Laurie, Charles Nelson Reilly, and Princeton University Library, guardian of the Zelda Sayre Fitzgerald papers. The play was originally commissioned by Lane Yorke.

William Luce
February, 1990

The Time:

March 10, 1948, the last day of Zelda Fitzgerald's life. She died in a fire that evening.

The Place:

The office of Zelda's psychiatrist, Robert S. Carroll, M.D., Highland Hospital, Asheville, North Carolina.

(The play is in two acts. All taped voices are recorded by the actress.)

Bye Bye Blackbird Copyright 1926 Warner Bros. Inc. (Renewed) by Mort Dixon & Ray Henderson. All Rights Reserved. Used by Permission.

Two Little Babes in the Wood Copyright 1928 Warner Bros. Inc. (Renewed) by Cole Porter. All Rights Reserved. Used by Permission.

I'm Goin' Crazy Copyright 1988 Stanart Music (ASCAP). Music & lyrics by Stan Freeman. All Rights Reserved. Used by Permission.

ACT I

Just before curtain, we hear Cole Porter's song, "Two Little Babes in the Wood".

AT RISE: ZELDA enters the dimly lighted office of Dr. Carroll. The MUSIC is interrupted by a loud-speaker announcement.

TAPED VOICE. (*As nurse.*) Attention, nursing staff. The recreation room is being painted, so please remind patients that the party tonight is in the cafeteria. I repeat, the party is in the cafeteria.

(*ZELDA is wearing an old dress and sweater. SHE carries a striped pillow case.*)

ZELDA. (*Looking around.*) Dr. Carroll? (*Surprised.*) He's not here. (*To audience.*) It's three o'clock, isn't it? (*SHE looks into the hall, then turns back to the room.*)

(*LOUDSPEAKER.*)

TAPED VOICE. (*As nurse.*) Nurse Holtzhausen, please call the main desk. Nurse Holtzhausen, call the main desk, please.

ZELDA. (*Opens the cigarette box on the desk. It plays "Clair de Lune."*) Luckies! I'll take some for George. (*To audience.*) This is just between us, okay? (*SHE crams cigarettes into her pocket, then listens to the music box.*) Dr. Carroll's theme song, "Clair de Loonie". (*Sitting, waiting.*) You know, it's strange, but I can't tolerate friends anymore. I can only tolerate enemies. You can see where that puts me. It makes me unfit to live in the world. Oh, well, what the hell. We're all iconoclasts, aren't we, in one way or another? (*Pause.*) Dr. Carroll, come out, come out, wherever you are.

(*LOUDSPEAKER.*)

TAPED VOICE. (*As nurse.*) Your attention, please. Dr. Carroll has been called away on an emergency. His afternoon appointments are cancelled.

ZELDA. (*Exultantly.*) Say that again!

(*LOUDSPEAKER.*)

TAPED VOICE. (*As nurse.*) Dr. Carroll's appointments are cancelled.

ZELDA. Hallelujah! No three o'clock inquisition! (*SHE checks the hallway. LIGHT-*

*ING change. SHE returns to the desk. With a
letter opener, SHE begins prying open the locked
file drawer of the desk.*) Thank you, Doctor, don't
mind if I do. (*SHE struggles with the lock until
SHE breaks open the drawer. To audience.*) Don't
ever fall into the hands of a psychiatrist, unless
you're feeling very Faustian. He'll destroy your
soul. (*Finding files.*) "Highland Hospital. Robert
S. Carroll, M.D. Confidential." (*Smiling.*) Not
anymore. (*Riffling through files.*) Here's
Katie's. All she does is wander around, yelling
... (*Rapidly.*) "Would somebody call me a cab?
Would somebody call me a cab?" (*More files.*)
Here's George's. (*Opening and reading.*)
"Permit patient the use of cosmetics on all but
visiting days." (*To audience.*) George is a long,
tall man who roams the halls in evening gowns.
He says his father wanted a boy, his mother
wanted a girl. I guess they were both satisfied.
(*More files.*) *"Fitzgerald, Zelda."*

(*ZELDA has found her own file. SHE puts the
other files away and begins to silently read
hers. Several beats. Angrily, SHE hurls her
file to the floor. Papers scatter everywhere.*)

ZELDA. (*Angrily.*) Can you tell me why in
the hell I should spend the rest of my life in this
place? I am sick to death of the repressive
atmosphere of sanitariums. It seems as though

I've been tidying up my room for years and not making noise in the halls. And I've climbed enough stairs to get to heaven. I just want to get as far away from Asheville, North Carolina, as I can. Mamma's always wanted me home with her, but Scott prefers dumping me in places like this. (*SHE picks up pages at random and then drops them. Singing.*)
>	Pack up all my care and woe,
>	Here I go, singin' low,
>	Bye Bye Blackbird.

(*SHE studies each page and lets it fall again. Her taped voice tells us what she is reading. SHE continues humming the song.*)

TAPED VOICE. (*As Zelda.*) "Fitzgerald, Zelda. Schizophrenic. Very slight progress. Patient rebels against authority, yet has been unable to function without institutional supervision for much of the past ten years. Do not stir up the patient. Relieve her of having to make decisions, which aggravates her disorder. Avoid confrontation, which is inadvisable at her stage of schizophrenia."

ZELDA. (*To audience.*) Excuse me for smiling. People think I've thought of something witty. The fact is, my smile is uncontrollable, and it terrifies me. (*Singing.*)
>	No one here can love or understand me,

Oh what hard-luck stories they all hand me. (*To audience.*) The fact is, I'm simply a neurotic woman who's reached the end of her physical resources and is exhausted. (*SHE picks up another sheet of paper from the floor and frowns as SHE reads it. Confidentially.*) Dr. Carroll doesn't know it, but I have a mission beyond these walls, a divine mission. I've got to tell the world a lot of things. Things about God and the end of the world and dying. (*Dropping the paper.*) But he won't permit me to talk about religion. Oh, hell, who cares, anyway? This generation is so spiritually dense, it thinks Armageddon is a new baking powder. And the religious majority still believes it's more commendable to suffer and repress than it is to walk the plank of adventure.

God help us. You have this little flickering light to shield from the world, to guide you out of the forest, and along comes a theologian and blows it out. (*SHE picks up another sheet of paper from the floor and peruses it. The information reminds her of the following.*)

I was always an excitement eater. When I was a child, I phoned the fire department. "Hello, Mr. Fireman? There's a little girl stuck on top of a house! The gray and white one at Six Pleasant Avenue. Hurry!"

I got the ladder, climbed onto the roof, kicked the ladder away and waited. The fire engine came clanging down the street, and the neighbors ran out to see what the hell was – (*Suddenly*

distracted, SHE drops the paper to the floor.) You
know something? Your arms look too long. And
your face is tiny and far away and out of
proportion. You look kaleidoscopic. (*Singing.*)

> I'm goin' crazy ... don't you wanna come
> along?

(*Pause.*) Do you know something else?
Nobody's ever sent me a get-well card. Isn't that
rotten? "Sorry you've gone insane, Zelda." Even
that would do. But not a word. (*SHE sits down and
picks up the pillow case.*) Isn't this lovely? It's
Highland Hospital's spring pattern.
"Penitentiary." (*Singing.*)

> I'm goin' crazy ... don't you wanna come
> along?
> Come and hear the cuckoo's song
> With me.
> Just like the loon bird,when he spreads his
> wings and soars,
> Headin' for those balmy shores
> We'll be.
> The world is riding toward that grand finale,
> But the trip is much more fun
> When you get off your trolley.
> So I'm goin' crazy ...
> Gonna join that daffy throng.
> Don'tcha wanna come along
> With me?

(*To audience.*) Don't look so smug. You're in
here with me, you know. (*SHE takes out her*

knitting, a bulky tangle of yarn with numerous holes from dropped stitches.)

(LOUDSPEAKER.)

TAPED VOICE. (*As nurse.*) Nurse Holtzhausen, would you please call the main desk? Nurse Holtzhausen, call the main desk, please.

ZELDA. Where the hell is Nurse Holtzhausen? Has anybody seen her? I wish *she'd* look tiny and far away. She checks my room every five minutes to see if I've strangled myself yet. I'm really rather angry that people won't let me be insane. I wish they'd accept me, without that feeling of having to acquit me. (*Knitting.*) Asheville's about as inspiring as leaky plumbing. Here, they've got me knitting this damned thing for therapy. Knit, purl, knit, purl, knit, purl. It's supposed to be a skirt. Ugly, isn't it? As you can see, my knits are fine. But my purls are so wide apart, I may have to use it for a fishnet. I think knitting's about as frolicsome as reading "Pilgrim's Progress." There's nothing good to read around here. Dr. Carroll chooses everything. Sometimes he brings old comic books ... when he's through with them. Here comes a purl. Wish me luck. (*Pause.*) I did it! Katie's making a crazy-quilt. K-K-K-Katie.

And I can't dance. They won't let me. "No dancing, Mrs. Fitzgerald." Now you talk about therapy. That could really help me. But Dr. Carroll says that's part of my problem. He and his goddamn feudal formulas. Just because my husband went and blabbed to him about Paris, and how I made myself sick going to ballet class eight hours a day. Scott couldn't realize that dancing was my refuge from the chaos in our lives.

Scott's refuge was the bottle. Do you know what they called him? "F. *Scotch* Fitzgerald." I guess there's nothing so indicative of civilization as the solaces people seek.

But I do hate the Teutonic sophistries of psychiatry. I'll probably never dance again. My muscles are getting so flabby, by the time I get out of here, if I ever do, my legs will look like Elsa Maxwell's. Though, during my last visit to Mamma's, I did start taking lessons again. But I had a quarrel with the teacher, Priscilla Billiejean Lillegard. I told Prissy I could not do steps that fit neither the period nor the spirit of the music.

(MUSIC begins. SHE takes off sweater and begins dancing.)

So I gave her some Schubert waltzes, hoping she'd choreograph them. But she apparently has impaired hearing. In fact, I told her so, and Prissy told me I was a cow. So I said she was a cow. And she said she couldn't be a cow if she tried. And I said, a cow doesn't have to *try* to be a cow — it just *is* one.

Oh, God, I wish I were back in Alabama this summer. The deep alfalfa fields and the low leaden moons and the frogs in the bullrushes. That lethal content and depth of poetry that hang over the South in summer. The tulip trees bowing in a thunderstorm. That haunting quality of dreariness, and no promise in the sky, and the trees dripping and the silver-mirrored river. Oh, the magic of it.

(*LOUDSPEAKER*)

TAPED VOICE. (*As nurse.*) Mister Crouse, please, your wife is at the desk. Mister Crouse, your wife is here.

(*ZELDA looks out the window.*)

ZELDA. I see George and Katie are playing croquet. (*Squinting.*) That dress looks like dotted Swiss. What a heavenly shade of blue. (*Pause.*) Katie's dress is pretty, too. (*Pause.*) She's yelling something. What's she saying? (*Listening.*) Oh, of course. (*Yelling.*) "Would somebody call me a cab? Would somebody call me a cab?" (*SHE leaves window. To audience.*) I wish they'd let us have animals here. Once I had this Persian cat named Chopin. His eyes were topaz. He was such a pretty cat. All white with furry boots. When he was still a kitten, he caught, tortured and ate his first mouse. So I gave him a coming out party of anchovies and cheese canapes.

After that initial triumph, he got more ambitious and tried to eat the parrot. Polly squawked so loudly, you could hear her five blocks away. There were feathers everywhere. After I spanked Chopin, he disappeared. Lost himself in Indian summer somewhere under the fallen leaves.

(*LOUDSPEAKER.*)

TAPED VOICE. (*As nurse.*) Mister Crouse, are you hiding? Your wife is here, *please.*

ZELDA. Oh, those Crouses. Sometimes I wonder which one of them lives here. (*Pause.*) When Polly wasn't scornfully eating peanuts, she was squawking, "Go to hell! Go to hell!" Daddy accused me of teaching her that. I told him it was Rosalind who did it. She's my sister. But he knew I was lying. Polly always sat next to the gramophone, and she knew all the latest songs. (*Singing, dancing.*)

Pack up all my care and woe,
Here I go singing low,
Bye Bye Blackbird.
Where somebody waits for me,
Sugar's sweet, so is he ...

Thank God, no Doctor Carroll today. No hypnotic heart-to-heart. What a relief. "Called away on an emergency." I'll bet. He's probably out on the golf course right now. (*SHE looks out the window, then picks up the phone. On phone.*) Tell the nurses' station, if they're still looking for Mr. Crouse — try the bushes near the parking lot. (*Drinking from Dr. Carroll's cup.*) Stale, but delicious. (*Looks in drawer.*) Oh, Dr. Carroll's bon-bons. (*Takes bite, scowls, puts it back.*) He won't even let me choose my own toothpaste. (*Finds lipstick in drawer.*) Katie's lipstick. Confiscated by Dr. Carroll. We're not allowed to use makeup. Only George. (*Putting it back; to audience.*) Has anybody got a candy bar? I'll trade you three Luckies for a Nutty Caramel. (*Shrugging.*) I don't like Baby Ruths. (*Pause.*) I'm sure Dr. Carroll thinks I'm incurably deranged. Yes, yes, he does. I know. I can tell by his manner. I can tell by his eyes. The unblinking eyes of a cobra. He thinks he can drive out the devils that are driving me.

(*During the following, ZELDA puts on Dr. Carroll's white jacket, which hangs on the back of his chair.*)

Every Wednesday at three P.M. it's the same routine. He puts on one helluva show. I come through that door and I say, "Dr. Carroll, have you talked with my mother? I want to go home for

Easter." (*As Doctor.*) Mrs. Fitzgerald, did you sleep well? (*To Doctor.*) No, I did not sleep well. Have you talked with my mother? I want to go home. (*As Doctor.*) Sit down, close your eyes and relax. (*To Doctor.*) Yes, Doctor. (*ZELDA obediently sits down. To audience.*) Every Wednesday, the same scenario. (*As Doctor.*) Feel your body relaxing. Feel yourself drifting. All extraneous thoughts are falling away. You are at peace. (*To Doctor.*) Yes, Doctor. (*To herself.*) God, how I hate that voice! (*As Doctor.*) As you drift deeper and deeper into a relaxed state, I want you to take a deep breath. Now. Take a deep breath and hold it. (*To audience.*) I think he's seen too many Basil Rathbone movies. (*As Doctor.*) Now slowly let the breath out. (*Pause.*) Again, a deep breath. (*Pause.*) Release the breath slowly. (*To audience.*) See what I mean about those eyes? (*As Doctor.*) Now, when I tell you, you will begin slowly counting backwards from one hundred. Begin. (*Zelda begins counting hurriedly. To herself.*) One hundred, ninety-nine, ninety ... (*As Doctor.*) Slowly. (*To herself, slowly.*) Ninety-eight, ninety-seven, ninety-six. Psychiatry's worse than witchcraft, I swear to God. It gives one the illusion of hope, when there isn't any. Ninety-five, ninety-four, ninety-three.

TAPED VOICE. (*As Mamma.*) Zelda! Zelda!

(*LIGHT change. She is now the young Zelda with a southern accent. She sheds the jacket and jumps up, extending her left hand.*)

ZELDA. (*To Mamma.*) Mamma! Oh, looka here. It's from Scott. (*Pause.*) It's an engagement ring, Mamma. What's it look like? It's his mother's. Isn't it grand? (*Calling.*) Rosalind! (*Pause.*) Oh, Mamma, I'm practically nineteen. (*To her sister.*) Rosalind, where's that card from Scott? (*SHE picks up another file page from the floor.*) Oh. Well, after this I'll thank you not to go snooping in my mail. (*To Mamma.*) Here, Mamma, you listen. (*Reading.*) "Darling, I am sending this just the way it came. I hope it fits, and I wish I were there to put it on your finger. I found a knockout apartment with a bathtub big enough for two." (*To Mamma.*) A bathtub, Mamma. In New York, everything's twice as big. (*Reading again.*) "Do write every day. So goodbye, my dearest sweetheart. Scott." (*The paper slips to the floor. Gazing at the ring.*) And it fits, Mamma. (*Dreamily.*) Mrs. Francis Scott Fitzgerald. It sorta says "soon" to me. Just sings it. Oh, just wait till I wear it Saturday night to the Country Club dance. Lurline Pearson's gonna turn absolutely green. (*Pause.*) 'Course, I'm going. I can't disappoint Frankie Stubbs. Besides, Scott's in New York, and I'm not letting being engaged stop me from having fun. Gosh, Eleanor Browder's engaged, and she's got more beaux than Solomon had wives. Why, if I get a chance, I'm gonna kiss all the bachelors in Alabama. If I haven't already. (*Pause.*) Nothing, Mamma. I was just spoofing. In the first place, I haven't kissed anybody. And in the second place, there's nobody left in the first place. (*SHE picks up another paper and begins writing on it at the desk.*) "Oh, Scott, my ring is so beautiful. Please, please don't be depressed. I'll come to you, lover, whenever you're ready. Don't you think I was made for you? I feel like you had me ordered and I was delivered to you to be worn. I want you to wear me like a watch, charm or buttonhole bouquet to the world. And then when we're alone, I want to help – to know that you can't do anything without me. You've trusted me with the dearest heart of all, and it's so damned much more than anyone else in the world ever had." (*Writing envelope.*) "From Zelda Sayre, Six Pleasant Avenue, Montgomery, Alabama." (*The paper falls back to the floor. She is now the present Zelda. To audience.*) Cradle of the Confederacy. We moved three times before settling there. Our neighborhood's called "The Hill." It used to be fancier. Just right for a State Supreme Court Judge and his family. A tidy, fashionable street. All the ladies and gentlemen of the town properly separated from their laundresses and butchers and charioteers of the ash cans. Even so, Mamma thought the ladies of the town were very provincial. She still does. Do you know, she's lived there for over seventy years?

TAPED VOICE. (*As Mamma.*) I'm not a native here, thank you very much.

ZELDA. She still won't admit to being part of Montgomery.

TAPED VOICE. (*As Mamma.*) Bottom rail's gettin' on top.

ZELDA. The neighborhood has changed. It's declined.

TAPED VOICE. (*As Mamma.*) Bottom rail's gettin' on top, I tell you, Zelda.

ZELDA. (*To Mamma, irritably.*) I know, Mamma! I know! (*To audience.*) Back of the house is Rosalind's room. My room's upstairs at the front. There. The window looks out on the old Wilson orchard. Oh, and there's a little white bed in the corner. In fact, the whole room's white. With the white curtains and all – it's like a hospital room (*To Doctor.*) Isn't *that* odd, Doctor? (*To audience.*) I remember when I was a little girl, I'd lie awake in the dark. The aroma of pears from across the way would fill my room. And as I'd fall asleep, I could hear a band playing waltzes in the distance. (*A slow, nostalgic waltz is heard briefly.*) I remember waking up early in those moated mornings, in those lost mornings. The sun all yellow and red, like a huge, luminous peach hanging ripe on a black shadow tree, just visible through the mist. There were amber squares of light across my bed. I'd be all sleepy-eyed, with cold toes and tangled hair, but I'd feel so clean and wholesome all day long, just because I saw the sun rise.

Especially in July I loved it, out in the picked cotton fields, the sky running red lava down the dirt roads, as if they were about to be buried under a furious glory.

Every place has its hours, don't you think? There's Rome in the glassy sun of a winter noon. There's Paris under a blue gauze of spring twilight. And there's a red sun flowing through the chasms of a New York dawn.

But in Montgomery in 1920, there was a time, a quality, that pertained to nowhere else. It began about half past six on an early summer evening, with the flicker and splatter of the corner street lights going on. And it lasted till the great incandescent globes were black with moths and beetles, and the children were called to bed from the dusty streets, and the grownups sat out on the porches, talking.

Who's from Montgomery? Anybody? (*Pause.*) Well, I remember. Time was tradition, and the past was actuality. (*Pause.*) Ninety-one, ninety, eighty-nine, eighty-eight.

TAPED VOICE. (*As Mamma.*) Zelda!

(*SHE reverts to being the young Zelda again. SHE takes Dr. Carroll's white jacket and puts it on backwards. In her mind, it becomes a dress in which she is being fitted.*)

ZELDA. (*To Mamma.*) Oh, Mamma, this'll be the prettiest wedding dress ever! It's like a cloud. (*Pause.*) Mamma, you can't imagine what a commotion my ring caused at the Club. Honestly, the whole dance was completely upset. And Lucy Goldthwaite told Theodosia Lee that – ouch! You stuck me. (*Pause.*) I *am* standing up straight! (*Pause.*) No, I don't want it that way. I want it to drop off the shoulder like this. See? (*Pause.*) It will too stay up! Jane Massey's wedding dress stayed up, and she's flatter'n an old pancake. (*Exasperated.*) Oh, Mamma! (*Hanging coat on chair.*) Then I'll wear my gray suit to be married in. Confederate gray. I may even bob my hair. I'll probably look like hell.

TAPED VOICE. (*As Daddy.*) Zelda!

ZELDA. Who's that calling my name? Daddy? (*SHE picks up another sheet of paper from the floor. It becomes a telegram*) Wait, Daddy! (*Reading telegram.*) Scott says we're gonna be married in St. Patrick's Cathedral, in the rectory. Just a few friends. Look, it's April third, the day before Easter. (*Dropping the paper.*) But, Daddy! (*To audience.*) Daddy gave me the trip north as a wedding present. He and Mamma didn't go to see me get married. Actually, they were glad the wedding was in New York, Scott being Irish Catholic and all. Daddy didn't approve of Scott, because he was a Princeton dropout, a drinker and a Yankee.

Mamma never made the dress. So I wore a suit of midnight blue, with a matching hat trimmed in leather ribbons and buckles. Scott adored it. (*Putting on sweater as if it were the new suit.*) When Daddy put me on the train for New York, he looked so handsome standing there, I was afraid I'd cry. (*To Daddy.*) G'bye, Daddy. (*To audience.*) That train pulled me out of the shadow-drenched land forever.

(*LOUDSPEAKER.*)

TAPED VOICE. (*As nurse.*) Attention, patients! Therapy Weaving Class in five minutes. Therapy Weaving in five minutes, Room 86.

ZELDA. (*Disoriented.*) Eighty-five, eighty-four, eighty-three ... (*Plucking at her sleeve.*) Where'd I get this ugly old thing? Looks like a gunny sack. (*Pause.*) They took away all my beautiful clothes. I used to have dozens of things with famous labels. Now they're all gone. Nurse Holtzhausen took them. (*To Doctor.*) *Your* orders, Dr. Carroll. (*To audience.*) Oh, well, I've gained too much weight to wear my old things. Look at these hips. The vulgarities of middle age have caught up with me. The insulin treatments have added twenty pounds. It embarrasses me.

Mamma sent me this dress. She made it a long time ago. It has what you might call a subtle lack of drama. It's very suitable for any occasion requiring discretion. I've had it so long, it's been in style three times. (*Holding up knitting.*) Well, at least I'll have a change of wardrobe when I finish this damned skirt. It looks enormous. I may end up giving it to Nurse Holtzhausen. What a Prussian intellectual she is. She wrinkles her brow when she reads "The Katzenjammer Kids."

In the winter, Nurse Holtzhausen wears a jacket of some indeterminate fur to work. In damp weather, it smells like a live animal. She says it's German mink. You ought to see it. If that's German mink, then somewhere in the Black Forest a muskrat's living under an assumed name. (*Imitating Nurse Holtzhausen, German accent.*) "I got to vork all mein life, Frau Fitzgerald. I vas not born mit a silver Löffel in mein mouth." (*Knitting; to audience.*) What a pity. That mouth could accommodate a service for six.

Nurse Holtzhausen says I need another permanent wave. What do you think? I suppose it does look a mess. The beautician comes today. Well, she's called the beautician, but she's really a local woman who shows up twice a week fried to the eyeballs. She does me on Friday. Her name is Iris McDougal, which is Greek for rainbow. Not the McDougal, just the Iris. She shampoos me and does a rather amateurish job of setting it.

Scott says when he first saw me in 1918, he thought my hair looked honey-yellow. I didn't color it, either. I remember the dress I was wearing. It was white silk with a chiffon tunic floating over it. And a large-brimmed hat as big as a manhole cover. And long streamers down my back. And a fan. Oh, my, a genuine Southern belle.

It was after my high school graduation. Scott was a first lieutenant at Camp Sheridan. I saw him standing at the edge of the dance floor, watching me waltz with Tommy Lee Culpepper.

I remember every soft spot of light that ever gouged a shadow beside his patrician bones. He was beautiful as men are not meant to be, with violet eyes and dark lashes and a straight nose and sensitive mouth. His hair was green-gold under the soft lights. Masculine beauty that I'd never seen before. And he was slightly but ecstatically intoxicated. (*Soft dance MUSIC begins.*) It was a radiant night of soft conspiracy. The dance floor was smoky with aspirations. (*To dance partner.*) 'Scuse me, Tommy Lee. (*To audience.*) I felt bodiless, like a phantom, as I moved into his waiting arms, without any introduction, a tender, inevitable gravity taking me and enfolding me there. (*SHE moves with the music.*) There seemed to be some heavenly support beneath his shoulder blades, that lifted his feet from the floor in ecstatic suspension. I thought he secretly possessed the ability to fly, but was dancing only as a compromise with convention. He whispered his name in my ear with a kind of alcoholic modesty.

(*The MUSIC fades out. SHE claps politely. Now the young Zelda, SHE becomes flirtatious.*)

ZELDA. (*To Scott.*) Francis Scott Fitzgerald? What a remarkable name. Are you related to Francis Scott Key, the man who wrote that awful song that nobody can sing? (*Pause.*) You are? Well, don't be offended, Lieutenant, but I hope it never becomes our national anthem. Woodrow Wilson's the only one who likes it, and he's such an ol' coot. *You* don't like it, do you? (*Pause.*) You *do?* Maybe I should listen to it a few more times with that in mind. (*Pause.*) My name is Zelda Sayre. Z-E-L-D-A. I got named after a gypsy queen in a novel Mamma was reading just 'fore she had me. (*Now the mature Zelda. To Doctor.*) Dancing with him, Doctor ... being close to him ... my face between his ear and his stiff army collar ... so clean and pure and dashing – oh, Scott, my golden god. (*To herself.*) Eighty-two, eighty-one, eighty. (*To Scott.*) Scott, why did you marry me? (*As Scott.*) Because you have some sense of the seriousness of life. (*To Scott.*) Seriousness? (*To audience.*) Me? (*To Scott.*) Why, I'm the original Flapper, my silly Goofo. I'm down there in black and white in your own novels as a proud and selfish little fool. There isn't a serious bone in my body. Remember? (*To audience.*) Once we drank ourselves blotto at a speakeasy. We bought a Rolls Royce as carelessly

as if it were a postage stamp, and I drove it back
home to Long Island, hitting all the fireplugs on
the way and Scott singing at the top of his lungs,
"Who'll Bite Your Neck When My Teeth Are
Gone?"

He started "Gatsby" then. It took him two
years to finish it. During that time, I woke from
my lethargy of sub-debism, I bobbed my hair, I lost
my Southern accent and I went into battle. I flirted
because it was fun to flirt. I wore a flesh-colored
bathing suit. Why? Because I had a good figure.
And I covered my face with powder and paint,
because I didn't need it. Do you know, I thought the
women in Botticelli's "Primavera" were ugly,
because they didn't look like the girls in the
Ziegfeld Follies?

I jumped into a fountain in my evening
clothes, and I rode down Fifth Avenue one hot
summer evening on top of a taxi. We both did. (*To
Scott.*) Didn't we, Scott? (*To audience.*) I was on
the hood and he was on the roof. That's how we met
Dorothy Parker. Smack in the headlights. "How
do you do, Miss Parker." (*To Scott, hurt.*)
Darling, look what she wrote about us! (*SHE picks
up another piece of paper from the floor. Reading.*)
"Contrived behavior, calculated to shock."
(*Dropping it.*) Well, we won't ask *her* Sunday!
(*Finding another paper.*) Scott, here's my list.
Let's see, the Calvin Coolidges, yes. And the
bathtub girl from Earl Carroll's Vanities and her
congressman. And Albert Schweitzer, yes. And

Harpo Marx. And the Archbishop of New York. And Tallulah Bankhead. Such good simple people, and all intimates of one another. (*Dropping the paper.*) We went to London once to see the fog, and saw Tallulah instead. (*Sitting on desk; toasting.*) Here's to the Flapper, who's growing old at last. She's come to none of the predicted bad ends, but has gone where all good flappers go – into marriage and boredom and convention and the unpleasant ordeal of having babies.

Who gives a damn about convention? Not me. The world isn't going to suffocate me. That's what this flapper's all about. Climb to the top and live high. And if the fine's a heavy one, what the hell!

I promise myself, if my poor soul comes starving and crying for bread, I'll eat the stone without complaint or remorse. There's only one act of significance. *You take what you want when you want it!* (*Pause.*) Oh, Jesus, did I believe that? (*SHE picks up another paper from the floor. Studying it.*) It says here, I was the last of six children. That's right. I was. My sisters and brother were much older. They weren't my playmates. So I played alone. (*Dropping the paper.*) I liked diving and climbing in the tops of trees. When I was a little girl, I liked jumping from high places. And I mean, *high* places. Like houses under construction. You know why? So I could run along the open roofs. I had complete confidence. I walked by myself against life. I didn't have a single feeling of inferiority or shyness or doubt. And no moral principles. (*To Doctor.*) I guess you could say, Doctor, that girl in the treetops was confident. (*Picking up a paper.*) Well, this is one helluva day, Doc. I think that word belongs in my file. (*Writing.*) *Confident.* (*SHE drops the paper.*)

TAPED VOICE. Mrs. Fitzgerald!

ZELDA. Seventy-nine, seventy-eight, seventy-seven. (*To reporter.*) So you're the gentleman from the Courier Journal. Won't you sit down? (*To Scott.*) Scott! Would you please come and help me be interviewed? The man from the newspaper is here! (*To reporter, charmingly.*) I've never been interviewed alone before. What do we do? Is it going to be very formal? (*Pause.*) No? Good. Shoot. (*SHE drinks from Dr. Carroll's cup.*) How do I prepare breakfast for my husband? Well, I ask the cook if there are any eggs. If so, I persuade her to poach two of them. (*Pause.*) Oh, yes, I adore sports. I've taken up golf. I play it exactly as Louis the Fourteenth did. On a stomach full of wine, I cheat a lot and I wear high heels. (*Pause.*) Yes, I love to write. You know, it's strange, but in my husband's last novel, I recognize excerpts from an old diary of mine that mysteriously disappeared after our marriage. And letters I wrote him, too. It seems our Mister Fitzgerald believes that plagiarism begins at home. (*To Scott.*) Scott, he wants to know whether we like large families or small? (*To reporter, shrugging.*) I don't know. (*SHE now drains Dr. Carroll's cup and slams it down on the desk. To Scott, demandingly.*) Scott, where's Philippe? We need more drinks. (*To reporter.*) Excuse me. (*Shouting.*) Philippe! (*To herself.*) Is it his day off? I don't remember. (*Shouting.*) Philippe! (*To reporter.*) Philippe's our butler. He must be taking his saxophone lesson. Actually, we've never heard him play. Just infrequent tootings from afar. (*Loudly.*) *Philippe!* Seventy-three, seventy-two, seventy-one.

(*Now distraught, ZELDA peers at the audience, then at the imagined Dr. Carroll.*)

ZELDA. (*To audience, bewildered.*) Why do I experience these eerie disorientations? (*To Doctor.*) Oh, Doctor, I wish I were that child again, climbing in those treetops. Dear God, that desperate nostalgia to be younger than young. It's so painful. (*To audience.*) Aren't you afraid of growing old? (*Pause.*) Neither was I. I used to say to myself, "Zelda, you'll be all right for another five years. You'll be pretty that long. It takes a good fifty years for time to batter down a woman's looks and crumple her charm." (*Gazing at reflection in decanter.*) Well, I was wrong. Look at me! The glamorous Mrs. F. Scott Fitzgerald and her Elizabeth Arden face – gone to pot. (*Putting down decanter.*) Now I know why Dr. Carroll removed all the mirrors. (*Pause.*) I'm glad Scott's gone. I wouldn't have wanted him to see me growing prosaic and wrinkled. Bitter things dried up behind my eyes. I've been physically and mentally ravaged by resentments, but I can't remember what they are.

I want to put my hands on something tangible, to be able to say, "This is real, this is part of my experience, this that happened to me is part of my memories."

There's one resentment I do remember. The time Scott made a fool of himself with Isadora Duncan. We'd gone to dinner in Saint-Paul-de-Vence, up above Nice, with Gerald and Sara Murphy. They had a villa there. They're very rich. Gerald wanted to be a painter, but he and Sara spent a good part of their lives then throwing a perpetual house party for the American caviar crowd.

Anyway, we were at dinner – some chicken thing – and there was Isadora Duncan sitting at a nearby table. Mind you, she was only forty-six, but she looked like an old woman. Very heavy. And her hair was dyed purple to match her dress. She looked ridiculous. And there were three silly young men hovering over her.

Before we knew it, there was Scott kneeling at her feet like some adolescent movie fan. You should've seen them. She leaned over, kissed his brow and ran her fingers through his hair. "My centurion," she said. "My handsome, brave centurion."

The old bag.

And then you know what she did? Invited him
to visit her room later that night. So I climbed on
top of the dining table – honest– and I leaped over
Gerald's head into the stairwell behind him, my
skirts flying. Watch out, everyone! Here I come!
(*Laughing.*) I skinned both my knees, ruined a
pair of silk hose – but it was one helluva show -
stopper! (*ZELDA laughs hysterically.*)

TAPED VOICES. Zelda ... Zelda ... Zelda.

(*SHE loses control and sinks into the chair,
trembling.*)

ZELDA. (*Soberly.*) Sixty-two, sixty-one, sixty.
Time is running out. I feel as though I've just
been born. That's how I feel. Born without a
family, without a friendly house about me, without
a scheme to settle into or rebel against. (*To
Mamma.*) Mamma, what was I like when I was
little?

TAPED VOICE. (*As Mamma.*) All my
children were good babies.

ZELDA. Oh, Mamma, that's not what I mean.
I've got no clear idea of what I was like. I feel like
I was nothing at all, and I don't know if I've
become myself yet, or if I'm still nothing. Did I
cry at night and raise hell, so that you and Daddy
wished I was dead?

TAPED VOICE. (*As Mamma.*) Zelda, what
an idea. All my children were sweet children.

ZELDA. Mamma, I don't want to hear about the others. I just want to know about me. Mrs. Kavanaugh always said she never saw a more troublesome child in her life than me. Is that true?

TAPED VOICE. (*As Mamma.*) Her little Clara was pigeon-toed and cross-eyed. Looked like her father. Jessie Kavanaugh was just envious.

ZELDA. But, Mamma, what was *I* like?

TAPED VOICE. (*As Mamma.*) Zelda, you were exceptional. All my children were exceptional babies.

ZELDA. (*Unsatisfied.*) Thank you, Mamma. (*To Doctor.*) Exceptional. Did you hear that, Doctor? (*SHE finds another piece of paper. Writing.*) Let's put that down. *Exceptional.* (*The paper drifts to the floor. To audience.*) Rosalind says I was Mamma's favorite. I was breast-fed till I was old enough to bite a chicken bone in two. Poor Mamma. (*Collecting all the cigarettes.*) Has anybody got a Charles Dickens book? I'll give you all of these for *Bleak House.* (*Pause.*) What am I talking about? That's what I've got. (*Pause.*) My head hurts. I feel like a somnambulist. Somnambulist. What a stupid word. In Montgomery, near the end of the war, the town was filled with soldiers from Camp Sheridan. There weren't enough girls to go around, so the not-so-pretty ones were dragged from their spinsterly pursuits to dance with the soldiers and make them feel at home. One evening, a nervous corporal asked Maggie Tuttle if she were a somnambulist. Dumb little Margie didn't know what the word meant, so just to be on the safe side, she slapped his face. (*To Doctor.*) No, Doctor, I don't want to talk anymore. (*Flaring.*) I *don't!*

(*SHE holds the cigarette box, as we hear "Clair De Lune."*)

ZELDA. (*Sighing with boredom.*) I know. Relax and continue counting backwards. All right. What comes after fifty-five? I don't mean after. I mean before. *Four*, that's it. Fifty-four, fifty-three, fifty-two, fifty-one. (*Sardonically.*) There's got to be a streak of sanity in me somewhere. Fifty. Why do we always have to count backwards? (*Opening eyes, to audience.*) I'll bet he plays golf from the ninth hole to the first. (*Closing eyes again.*) Forty-nine, forty-eight.

END OF ACT I

ACT II

Just before rise, we hear the MUSIC BOX playing briefly. It is interrupted by the LOUDSPEAKER.

TAPED VOICE. (*As nurse.*) Attention. Those interested in Dr. Dewey's nature walk, meet at the south entrance in forty-five minutes. Wear comfortable shoes. Wear comfortable shoes, please.

(*LIGHTS up on ZELDA. SHE is still in the chair, her eyes closed. SHE continues the countdown.*)

ZELDA. Forty-five, forty-four. The cradle rocks on in the continuous lullaby of recapitulation. (*To Doctor.*) Oh, Doctor, I seem so queer to myself. I look out the window and see humanity as a bottle of ants, and I lose control. (*As Doctor.*) Say anything that comes to mind, Mrs. Fitzgerald. (*To Doctor.*) Okay. Scott and I lived in a big house by the river. Wilmington. (*Opening her eyes.*) Wait a minute. This isn't Wilmington. Where the hell am I? (*Pause.*) Oh, Ellerslie. (*Settling back.*) Ellerslie, it was called.

On the banks of the Delaware. We lived in the
cinders and wind from the river. And sometimes,
rarely, we did things together. Yet we were happy
there. We didn't seem to care very much whether
we were happy or not. I suppose we expected
happiness was going to be something more
dramatic. (*A new memory.*) Doctor Carroll, do
you see those ornaments? We dragged them out
every year since I was a little girl. (*Amused.*)
"*What* ornaments?" Close your eyes, Doctor,
count backwards, and maybe *you'll* see them, too.
The Christmas tree ornaments! Maybe you and I
should trade places. They're birds of paradise
with spun glass tails. And those little silver bells
that ring through the night all by themselves. (*To
audience.*) Do you know, once I walked into a
Christmas cotillion, and butlers and footmen fell
about me like a flurry of early snow? And I asked
myself what it was that gave me such
instantaneous authority? Being Mrs. F. Scott
Fitzgerald?

One smart old lady at the cotillion said, "As
far as I can see, she's just a cheeky little flapper
with clean ears." (*SHE picks up a sheet of paper
and looks at the writing on it.*) Oh, yes, I
remember. We had a maid, Marie, a wonderful
Negro girl. She was high and gawky. She
laughed and danced barefoot around the tree on
the broken ornaments. She didn't seem to notice.
What an incredible spirit. (*Pause.*) And there
was Philippe. (*Trying to remember.*) Philippe?

Oh, yes. With the saxophone. Scott found him in a
Paris gymnasium, and over my objections
brought him home to America to be his drinking
companion and chauffeur. I guess it was hard to
find chauffeurs in Delaware. They were all in
Congress.

Philippe had a handsome, Bacchanalian face.
He was a Parisian weight-lifter and a taxi-
driver. He wanted to run the house like a Paris
taxi-cab. He was always flexing his muscles and
shadow-boxing. I think he had blocked too many
punches with his head. He and Scott were always
grappling with each other. Actually, his official
capacity in the house was that of butler. We called
him in from the kitchen with a French taxi horn. I
guess it kept him from feeling homesick, the little
shit.

And there was Ella, who sang spirituals in the
kitchen. (*Dropping the paper.*) And when thunder
blew up the Maryland lightning belt at night and
whipped and crackled over the river, Ella sat like
a dark ejection of the storm in the candlelight of
the dining room, singing in a quavering voice.
(*Singing.*)
Swing low, sweet chariot,
Comin' for to carry me home.

(*SHE picks up another paper from the floor. SHE
scans it curiously.*)

ZELDA. And then there was Max. Max Perkins, my husband's editor. (*To Doctor.*) Doctor, he once said ... (*Reading.*) "Zelda is a girl of great character." (*Dropping paper.*) Yes, he did. And there was William Wreford. (*Pause.*) W-R-E-F-O-R-D. Once I skipped school and spent a day in the graveyard, trying to unlock a rusty vault built into the side of a hill. It was all washed and covered with weepy, watery blue flowers that might've grown from dead eyes, sticky to touch and with a sickening odor. The boys wanted me to get into the tomb to test my nerve, and I wanted to sense the man who was buried there. (*Thoughtfully.*) William Wreford, 1842. Forty-one, forty. Why should graves make people feel in vain? I've heard that so much. I can't find anything hopeless in having lived. All the broken columns and clasped hands and doves and angels mean romance. And in a hundred years, I think I shall like having young people speculate on whether my eyes were brown or blue. Of course, they're neither. Death is so beautiful, so very beautiful. (*The spell is now broken.*) More? Goddamn it, Doctor, you're never satisfied! More, more, more! (*SHE grabs a handful of papers from the floor.*) Here. Over the years I've put together twelve scrapbooks. Photographs and clippings and things, telling us what wonderfully mediocre people we were. (*Discarding a paper.*) Here's one of me when I was five. And there's Mamma. And I'm holding Patsy. I had a red wagon and a rag doll named Patsy, and I pulled her around in it. (*Discarding another.*) And that's Daddy. "The Brains of the Bench." That's what they called him. Always wore a fedora. He was forty-two years old when I was born. That's too old. (*Discarding another.*) That's me with Speck Shaffer. We were sixteen and all dressed up for a dance. I made him stay out half the night. When we got home, Daddy was waiting up. (*As Daddy, angrily.*) Do you know it's four o'clock in the morning, you little hussy? (*To Daddy, demurely.*) Why Daddy, is that not the time when all hussies come in? (*To Doctor.*) Look at Daddy standing there, abstract and proud, rocking back and forth from his toes to his heels. (*To Daddy.*) Daddy, do you remember the first day that Scott came to dinner? (*To audience.*) He's forgotten. How very convenient. (*To Daddy.*) Well, I haven't. (*As Daddy, outraged.*) Zelda! You're too big to sprawl on Mr. Fitzgerald's lap. (*To audience.*) That's how it started. (*To Daddy.*) Oh, Daddy, it's no one's goddamned business what I do. (*As Daddy.*) Zelda! I forbid you to blaspheme in this house! (*To Daddy.*) Goddamn, goddamn, goddamn! (*To audience.*) Well, he flew into a rage. (*As Daddy.*) You corrupt little hussy! Look at you, paint all over your face! Go wash it off this instant! (*To Daddy.*) Goddamn, goddamn, goddamn! (*To audience.*) Poor Daddy. Well, I mean, it was poor Scott. That was his introduction to the Sayre family. (*To Daddy.*) G'night, Daddy.

(*To audience.*) Do you know, "Old Dick" goes to bed at eight o'clock every night? Boring!

(*SHE plays hopscotch as the young Zelda.*)

    ZELDA. (*Chanting.*)
Close up the window,
And open up the door,
We're gonna have a dance
On the kitchen floor!
Anga, panga, eep, ip, ohp!
Anga, panga, eep, ip, ohp!
(*Excitedly.*) My turn! I'm it!

(*SHE hides behind the desk.*)

    ZELDA. Thirty-five, thirty-four, thirty-three, thirty-two, thirty-one ...
    TAPED VOICE. (*As Mamma.*) Zelda!
    ZELDA. Mamma, do I have to come in already? It isn't even dark yet.
    TAPED VOICE. (*As Mamma.*) Zelda!
    ZELDA. (*SHE flops in the chair, crossing her legs.*) Here it comes. The "No Ladies Code of Conduct."
    TAPED VOICE. (*As Mamma.*) Zelda ...
    ZELDA & TAPED VOICE. (*As Mamma.*) No lady ever sits with her limbs crossed.
    ZELDA. (*Uncrossing legs.*) You mean my legs, Mamma?

ZELDA & TAPED VOICE. (*As Mamma.*) No lady ever uses the word "legs." The word is "limbs." You may cross your ankles, but not your limbs. Moreover, no lady ever allows her back to touch the chair. No lady ever steps out the front door without fastening her gloves. And no lady ever lets her bare feet touch the floor. We are genteel Southern ladies, and don't you forget it.

ZELDA. No, Mamma. (*To audience, disdainfully.*) Genteel Southern ladies. The Southern belle was created by the Southern man as a stereotype to flatter his ego. When she says hello, she's told you everything she knows. A baby face with a brain to match. You know the type. Small intellect and tiny interests. She goes through life with a languishing death-bed air. And despite the fact that nine out of ten Southern ladies do not die tomorrow or the next day, she gives the impression of being an imminent martyr. The noble Southern women I've known would abhor that attitude in anyone.

Once I went to a dance at which the college men recited a pledge by torchlight. (*Standing, hand over heart.*) "To the Southern Belle, paragon of unblemished beauty, we dedicate our lives and honor in the protection of her sacred virginity."

After that ludicrous ceremony, I made Irby Jones dance cheek to cheek with me, to the horror of the chaperones. Sometimes after dances, we'd sneak out to the cars for a little boodling. Boodler's Bend. That's where we parked for necking. In the pecan orchard at the end of Court Street.

And down that way, Lloyd Hooper and I used to park the car across the street from Mrs. St. Clair's brothel, and I'd turn the car lights on all the boys we knew, as they went skulking up the front steps. (*Teasingly.*) There's Char-lie! Charlie Mosley! I see you! Beep, beep! (*To audience.*) Daddy didn't always know what was going on, and Mamma was afraid to tell him. If he told me I couldn't go out, I just climbed out the window and I went. Anga, panga, eep, ip, ohp. (*To Doctor.*) Yes, Doctor, I had a bad reputation.

TAPED VOICE. (*As teacher.*) Zelda, turn around and stop talking.

ZELDA. What?

TAPED VOICE. (*As teacher.*) Girls, get out your assignment.

ZELDA. My assignment? (*To audience.*) Oh, it's my high school English teacher, Harriet Beecher Witherspoon. Miss Witherspoon was a spinster lady. Her face was white and pink with ante-bellum cosmetics.

TAPED VOICE. (*As teacher.*) Your assignment was to write a poem on love, in its loftier and more spiritual aspects. Eleanor Browder, would you begin?

ZELDA. (*As Eleanor.*) Yes, Miss Witherspoon. (*Reading.*)

How sweet, how pure, is mother love,
With ministrations kind,

Unselfish as the day is long,
With wisdom unconfined.

(*SHE sits down.*)

TAPED   VOICE.   (*As   teacher.*)   Very
acceptable. And now, Theodosia Lee, your poem,
please. And do stand up straight, dear.
    ZELDA. (*As Theodosia. Standing, reading.*)
Because God loved the world so much,
He gave His only Son,
May I be worthy of His love
Before my life is done.

(*SHE sits down.*)

TAPED VOICE. (*As teacher.*) Excellent,
Theodosia. Now, Zelda Sayre, let us see if you can
add the perfect gem to our diadem of poesy.
Proceed, Zelda.
    ZELDA. (*Standing.*) Yes, Miss Witherspoon.
(*Reading enthusiastically.*)
I do love my Charlie so,
It nearly drives me wild,
I am so glad that he's my beau,
And I'm his baby child!
    (*Tossing paper in air.*) Put that in your
diadem, Miss Witherspoon!

(*LOUDSPEAKER.*)

TAPED VOICE. (*As nurse.*) Attention, ladies. Miss McDougal has had car trouble. She asks that you shampoo each other, and she will set you when she arrives. I repeat, you will shampoo each other.

ZELDA. (*Mouthing words.*) Shampoo each other? (*To audience.*) I had a bad reputation, all right. I smoked rabbit tobacco in a corn-cob pipe, and if there wasn't any gin, I drank corn liquor cut with coke. Mamma said, "If you've added liquor to your tobacco, you can subtract your mother. The habits of a prostitute do not mix with Southern gentility." (*To Mamma, quietly.*) Yes, Mamma. (*To audience.*) In Montgomery there was this ice-cream parlor on Dexter Avenue. Harry's Place. It was the local jelly joint. All the boys gathered there. I called them my "Jelly Beans." They just loafed around. You know how boys do when they don't have dates. Once they drove by the house, yelling my name.

TAPED VOICES. Zelda! Zelda! Zelda!

ZELDA. I ran out on the veranda. (*Calling.*) My Jelly Beans! All my beautiful Jelly Beans! I love you! (*To audience.*) Daddy was home and he was livid. He said,"Your personal conduct is outrageous! How dare you make a spectacle of yourself!" (*To Daddy.*) I don't care. I've got a right to do anything I want! (*As Daddy.*) People who do not subscribe have no rights! (*To audience.*) And that was Daddy, the judge. (*Furtively waving.*) G'bye, my Jelly Beans. (*To herself.*) It's too damned hot to dance. (*To Doctor.*) You still there, Doctor Carroll? With your goddamned clipboard and fountain pen, taking down everything I say. You think you can put Humpty-Dumpty back together again? I've got news for you.

Oh, for the good old days of Confederate manure and uniforms to match. That's what Mamma thinks. I wonder why?

Did you ever play "Wonder Why?" (*Pause.*) Yes, Doctor, it's called "Wonder Why." I play it all the time. I wonder why I like it here? Nothing ever happens. I grew up on the infinite promise of American advertising. I wonder why I still believe you can learn to play the piano by mail, or that mud will give you a perfect complexion?

Oh, no, no, I don't. I'm neither young enough nor credulous enough to think you can manufacture something out of nothing, to replace the song I once had. I just want to go home. But Mamma's world is over there. Too far to reach now. Just a dream in a memory-laden town.

Don't try to fool me, Doctor. I know I'm looking into abstract time. Life is slowly receding, and it's leaving me stranded. I wonder why I'm not what I thought I was? I'm so tired. I'd have collapsed years ago if I'd had me on my hands. (*Pause.*) No, Doctor, I do *not* want to talk about my husband. (*SHE picks up a piece of paper and peruses it.*) Anyway, he's dead. (*Reading.*) "He died eight years ago. A heart attack in

Hollywood." (*Dropping the paper.*) Scott was the keynote and prophet of his generation. The Jazz Age. And – and – (*SHE gropes for the next idea.*) And I'm so fed up with these wistful, tragic silhouettes of Scott and Zelda. People want to bank on gods? Well, that's too bad! He came home last night and he smashed me in the nose. He broke down the bathroom door and punched me in the nose. (*Nervously, she changes the subject.*) Doctor Carroll, do you know where I'd like to be right now? With Scott on the roller coaster, yelling our fool heads off. The Big Dipper! Yaay! You know where else I'd like to be? You guess. (*Removing sweater.*) *Alabama?* Good God, no! On the beach at St. Raphael on the Riviera. Just sleeping together, covered with the flakes of dried salt water on a July afternoon. (*To audience.*) You can tell I'm a sensualist. (*SHE lies down, as if sunning herself.*) It was as close to paradise as we ever got. It was like a transfusion of light. It was also monotonous. Scott was so irritable – so remote. He left me entirely to myself. So much being wasted, I thought. Pine groves and gardens dropping into the sea. You can't force a soul to feel fidelity, can you? The realization that the ties in which you've invested so much are perishable, is terrifying.

And so, Edouard came into my life. His hair, the gold of a Christmas coin. Broad bronze hands. Kissing him was like embracing a lost religious rite. (*Putting on sweater; to Edouard.*) I hope Scott didn't see us. Do you think he did? I should tell him. I'll have to. I don't know. (*Picking up papers; to audience.*) "It would be unwise," he said. "We must hold onto our benefits." Some benefits. An eleven-by-fourteen glossy of himself. And that's not all. He left a letter in French, which I couldn't read. (*Ripping up papers.*) So I tore it up. I tore up the picture, too. What was the use of keeping them? There's never been a way to hold onto summer.

Edouard got himself transferred to Indo-China. Whatever it was I wanted from him, he took it with him to squander on the Chinese. And the strange thing is – nothing really happened. No, it didn't. Scott would never believe it, but Edouard and I only talked of love. Mind you, I'm not a monogamist in theory – only in practice.

There are all kinds of love in the world, but never the same love twice. Scott wrote that once. If only I could see him one more time. And yet, there'd be nothing to greet him but an empty shell. (*To Scott.*) Had I any feelings, dearest, always dearest Scott, they'd be in gratitude to you and in sorrow that of all my life, there should not be even the smallest relic of the love and beauty we started with to offer you at the end. (*To audience.*) I still look down every track and I see Scott coming. Out of every haze and mist, I see his dear rumpled trousers hurrying toward me. I remember the rough edges of his cuffs, and the neatness of his worn possessions, and how he smelled of pencils and tweed. His lazy agitation when he dressed.

I see him walking on a balcony, absent-mindedly dropping a cigarette and standing poised in the morning sun. And I'm perpetually amazed that he's so handsome. I want to shut him up in a closet, like a dress too beautiful to wear.

If he were in my bed tonight, it might be the back of his head I'd touch, where the hair is short and mossy. Wherever I touch, it would be the sweetest place in all the world. Stretching our legs down beside one another and feeling all warm and hidden in the bed, like seeds beaten into the earth.

TAPED VOICE. (*As Mamma.*) Zelda, no lady ever discusses the private intimacy of – er – well, no lady ever discusses it, that's all.

ZELDA. Yes, Mamma. I know. No lady ever discusses it. (*Slapping her arm.*) Damned mosquitoes. (*Staring offstage.*) I see Mr. Kavanaugh's out in his dirty undershirt, watering his moon vines. That's odd. I thought he died years ago. (*Pause.*) Wait a minute. He *did* die. I don't get it. (*To Doctor.*) Doctor, would you explain that illusion? And what about this noise in my ears? (*Pause.*) Well, why in the hell can't you cure me? I am so confused. There's nothing kinetic inside me. No internal force, I have to be led or driven. And I'm cold, so cold. And I forget where I am. Some hospital. Highland Hospital, that's it. Room 29. (*Pause.*) Twenty-eight, twenty-seven, twenty-six.

Before I realized I was sick in Paris, there was a new significance to everything. Stations and streets and facades of buildings. The colors were infinite. It was like walking with a child beside me, the air was so tender. And there was music that beat behind my forehead. I danced and danced. Eight hours a day. With Madame. Because I was miserable with Scott and his endless parties and nothing else. (*To Scott, angrily.*) Not Gertrude Stein's again! And what am I supposed to do while you're worshiping at her big feet? Sit in the other room with those gaunt creatures with no eyebrows, and listen to Alice Toklas hold forth? (*Pause.*) Well, you should see yourself listening to her with that same gaping look that sinners have, when they hear the Lord's Prayer! As if she were some major prophet! To me, she's just a dumpy old woman with a haircut like a French barber's. (*To audience.*) I remember once in her studio, Miss Stein complimented a young poet on his work, and he vomited from sheer emotion all over her priceless Tibetan prayer rug. (*Picking up mug.*) Who's this from? (*Reading.*) "To Scott and Zelda from Gertrude and Alice." (*Putting it down.*) Wonderful. Just what I need. A shaving mug. Merry Christmas. (*To Doctor.*) Do you know what I want for Christmas, Doctor? A cowboy belt with bright stones and brass nails, size twenty-eight. And a pair of beaded leather moccasins, size five. And a vial of perfume, and ... (*Emotionally.*) We

weren't just   happy once! We were happy a
thousand times! (*Pause.*) Here's to Christmas,
1925! Twenty-four, twenty-three, twenty-two,
twenty-one. You'd think he could've come to visit
me for Christmas. Just for a few days. After all,
there isn't forever left to either of us. I wonder if
he'll ever come East again.

He says I've failed him. Well, it's just barely
possible he's failed me, the sonuvabitch. I'm no
fool. I've seen her. A simpering Hollywood
starlet.

Lois. She's like breakfast food. No definite
characteristic of her own. She revels in attention
from men, and enjoys the rumor going around
that she has the most beautiful blue veins all over
her little body.

"Lolo." Well, nobody ever had a more
symmetrical body to help her to stardom. It's like
an impersonal mechanical installation.

I wonder why men never seem to become the
things they do. And they're always needing
babying about their sexual desirability. (*To
Scott.*) No, Scott, I am not reproaching you. I
simply would like to know why, when you saw in
Paris that I was sick and sinking, you sat in the
bathtub and sang "Play in Your Own Backyard?"

And my dancing you hated. And my love for
Madame. Why? You had Hemingway and his
crowd. And you blamed me when you couldn't
write, when you know the real reason was you
were out half the night with the boys, drinking

yourself unconscious. (*SHE pursues Scott around the desk.*) No, goddamn it, you let me finish! You whined about your lonely struggle against gifted and talented writers, and how I was only a third-rate writer and a third-rate ballet dancer. If that was true, then why the hell did you put your name on my short stories? Why did you help yourself to my diaries and letters?

And twice that summer you left our bed saying, "I can't! Don't you understand? I can't!" (*Pause.*) Oh, Scott, it didn't matter, that part of it. Believe me, it didn't matter. If only we'd been close in other ways. (*To Doctor.*) He told me once that he married me because I had some sense of the seriousness of life. Now I see he was right. You see, I believed in love, which made me the stable person in the marriage. (*Picking up paper.*) That should go in my file, Doctor. (*Writing.*) *Stable.*

TAPED VOICES. Help! Help! Help!

ZELDA. (*Dropping the paper.*) Did you hear that?

TAPED VOICES. Help! Help! Help!

ZELDA. I used to hear voices only once in awhile, but now I hear them all the time. Out of the walls, up the drain pipes. "Help!" they cry. (*Impatiently.*) Oh, I know they're inside me! Don't you think I know that? But I had this dream. I was asleep on the top floor of an insane asylum — in my dream, I mean — it was a bright, garish room filled with smoke, and Scott was above me on the roof, calling to me. "Zelda!" And I woke up. In my dream, I mean.

TAPED VOICE. (*As Scott.*) Zelda! Zelda! Zelda!

ZELDA. (*Screaming.*) Scott! I'm down here! (*To audience.*) And I run! I run into the hallway. All the guards have left, and the patients are outside my door, grinning at me and beckoning me to join them. They're so grotesque, it frightens me. I pull away. I run back into my room, screaming. (*To Scott.*) Scott, I'm here! (*To audience.*) And I hear Scott calling, "Zelda! Don't be insane!" (*To Scott.*) Scott! Come and get me! Please, come and get me! (*ZELDA crumples up, sobbing. To audience.*) Nobody, not even the poets, can measure how much a heart can hold. But hearts perish in public institutions. (*Singing softly.*)

Oh, Susanna,
Oh, don't you cry for me,
I come from Alabama
With my banjo on my knee.

(*Pause.*) Well, since I've come this far alone, I suppose I can go the rest of the way. (*SHE begins sketching on her drawing pad.*) Save yourself, Scott. Don't worry about the rest of the world. Play in your own backyard.

"Save yourself." The immortal words of the great Ernest Hemingway. How like Ernest. I always questioned Scott's attachment to Ernest. Mencken says it was the oddest infatuation he ever saw. Bob McAlmon told Morley Callaghan that Ernest is a fairy. So, I said to Scott, "Bob McAlmon is certainly in a position to know. If it isn't true, why doesn't Ernest sue him?"

"Leave him alone!" Scott would yell at me. "Say anything you please, but lay off Ernest!" (*To Scott.*) Well, excuse me. (*SHE picks up another sheet of paper from her file. To audience.*) Do you see this review from Time Magazine. (*Reading.*) "Jazz Age Priestess Brings Forth Paintings." That's me. (*Pause.*) I'll bet you didn't know I had exhibitions in New York and the Montgomery Art Museum. That was a year ago. (*Reading.*) "The work of a brilliant introvert, vividly painted, intensely rhythmic." (*Dropping paper.*) I hear Ernest came to see the New York exhibit. I wonder what he thought? (*Shrugging.*) Oh, who gives a shit? (*SHE studies her sketch. To Doctor.*) Doctor, do you equate emotions with colors? I do. Pale orchid is aspiration. Vermillion is passion. And jade is jealousy. (*To audience.*) Scott said I was jealous of Ernest. But it wasn't that. The first time we met, Ernest took Scott aside and told him I was crazy. Scott thought it was so funny, he repeated it to me. I didn't laugh. And I hate the constant effort of pulling punches. So, I said it ... (*To Scott.*) He's a pansy with hair on his chest! (*To audience.*) And that was just the beginning! (*To Scott.*) Ernest Hemingway is as phony as a rubber check, and you know it – tearing me down and borrowing money from you while he does it. The

big bogus. And I don't like the way you two haunt
the male bars on the Left Bank and drag us along.
What's the matter? You need wives for courage?
(*Pause.*) I won't shut up! He's a swaggering bore,
trying to prove his masculinity. Imagine
crossing a street and beating up on a poor,
effeminate young man – a perfect stranger – just
to show his virility! The big war hero, the tough
guy, game-hunting, bull-fighting, bull-slinging!
Bull-shit! (*Pause; to audience.*) I believe there's
an Actuality. (*To Scott.*) I know what you call it,
Scott. You call it God. I call it Beauty. We're
evolved from Eden, you and I. And let's face it, the
impulse of homosexuality is as old as God. Are
you listening to me, Scott? It's as much a part of the
Actuality as anything else from the Beginning. I
wish you'd believe me, because of your artist's
soul, and not be so afraid. Do you understand
anything of what I'm saying? (*To audience.*) Do
you? That Beauty perfects us through many lives,
through subtle changes of gender, till we attain
self-completeness. And at last – no, again – we
inherit the Paradise we never lost. Life shimmers
over us. Don't you see it? A divine afflatus. Here.
Now. And what I understand, what you
understand, becomes our spiritual property.
Then, why do we visit abuses on our fellow man
because of his differences? (*Pause.*) I had this
friend in ballet class. She was so lovely and
quiet. Ordinarily, women bore the tar out of me. I
think she was a lesbian. (*Confidentially.*) Here

in Highland Hospital, we're not allowed to use that word. (*Hollering into hallway.*) *Lesbian!* (*To Doctor.*) I'll show you this masterpiece in a minute, Doctor. (*To audience.*) I remember one night, Scott came home after being with Ernest. And in his sleep, he moaned, "No more, baby, no more."

No more, baby? Good God, suspicions are awful. I torture myself with this, because – I don't know why. If I did, I wouldn't be stuck in this nut house, knitting fishnets and drawing this – (*SHE shows the sketch to the doctor.*) I call it "Love." Well? (*SHE shows it to the audience. To audience.*) Well? (*Pause.*) No one said you had to like it! (*To Doctor.*) Is it the title you don't like? Because I can change it, if there's something you'd like better. (*SHE puts the drawing away.*) I shall exhibit my soul no longer. (*Pause.*) Oh, Doctor, I want to thank you for moving me into my new room. Even though the bathroom's a bit strange. It was altered for a lady who was too fat to climb in a normal tub or sit on a normal commode. But I like the high windows. That way, I can look out at the sky. Do you know "Oedipus," Doctor? (*SHE looks up, transfixed.*)

We saw of old blue skies and summer seas
When Thebes in the storm and rain
Reeled, like to die.
O, if thou can'st again,
Blue sky – blue sky!
TAPED VOICES. Zelda! Zelda!

ZELDA. There's a cat crying in the hedge.
Here, kitty, kitty. (*SHE looks for it.*) I thought it
was Chopin, but it isn't. Poor Chopin, with a heart
like a honeywell. I never saw him after I spanked
him. Then we got this black cat, but we had to take
her back, because she had diarrhea. Then we got
this dog from the city pound. We called him Ezra
Pound.

Where do you think animals go when they
die? I think they're as good as people. Better. They
deserve to go to heaven more than we do.

I saw Daddy die, and I wasn't afraid of going
myself. After all, death is the only real elegance.

(*SHE rummages among the papers for a phone
number, then goes to the phone and dials.*)

ZELDA. (*On phone.*) Operator? I want to send
a telegram to Scott Fitzgerald. Hotel Christie.
Hollywood. "Daddy died last night. Stop. Don't
worry about us. Stop." Bill it to Garfield 7-0-0-9.
(*Hanging up the phone.*) Eight, seven. (*To
Daddy.*) Oh, Daddy, there are so many things I
wanted to ask you. (*To audience.*) Would you look
at him? He's so frail. I wonder how he fed us all.
"Baby," he said, "was there somethin' you wanted
to ask me?" (*To Daddy, words tumbling out.*) Oh,
yes, Daddy! Can you tell me why, when our bodies
ought to bring relief from our tortured minds, they
fail and collapse? And why, when we're
tormented in our bodies, does our soul desert us as

a refuge? Why do we spend years using up our bodies to nurture our minds with experience, only to have our minds turn to our exhausted bodies for solace? Why, Daddy, why? (*To audience.*) You know what he said? "Baby, ask me somethin' easy."

Daddy left me nothing but his high principles and his doubts. After he died, I went looking through his papers for another legacy. All I found was a mildewed purse containing three nickels. It was the first money Daddy ever made. Oh, Daddy.

It's just the little personal things we care about in people. Who cares what good or evil dies? God is always ready to forgive. That's why it seems right that I forgive Daddy's indifference to me, just as I hope some day to be forgiven by my own dau– (*Pause.*) My own daughter. (*Angrily.*) I don't want to play this morbid little game anymore! I want to wake up! (*SHE gathers her things and starts to leave. At door.*) No, Doctor, I can't. (*Pause.*) Please. (*Pause.*) She called me Mommie when she was little. I remember, I looked out the window at Ellerslie, and there was this lone and lovely child knocking a croquet ball through the arches of summer, under the chestnut tree. And that night, I heard her singing alone in her bed, in a house too immense and chaotic for a child. (*To Scottie.*) Scottie. So like your Daddy, with that horizon quality in your eyes. In Paris, we bathed you in the bidet by mistake. And once, at lunch, you gulped down a gin fizz, thinking it was lemonade. I loved your thin child's legs and your suspended-in-motion way of walking. And when I kissed you, there was that little school-child scent at your neck.

Oh, Scottie, my baby, be strong and happy. For you I'll make the jasmine bloom and all the trees come out in flower. We'll eat clouds for dessert and bathe in the foam of rain. And I'll make you a new dress from a blue hydrangea bush and shoes from pecan shells, and I'll sew you a belt from leaves. Just we three together. We'll have a little house with hollyhocks and a green apple tree. And you'll be running somewhere in Renoir, and your Daddy will be writing dozens of books, and — (SHE breaks down. To audience.) What are you staring at?

TAPED VOICES. Mrs. Fitzgerald! Mrs. Fitzgerald! Mrs. Fitzgerald!

ZELDA. Yes, yes, yes, yes, yes! *Mrs. Fitzgerald!* That's all I ever was! I never had an identity without *Mr.* Fitzgerald. At least, when I was with Scott, I had someone to butt my vitality against, so it didn't litter the air like sprays of dynamite.

Then after he abandoned me here, he became furious when he found out I'd sent my first novel to Max Perkins without consulting him. Do you know what he told Max? "I'm going to edit her book." And he tore the heart out of it, because he said my life was his literary domain.

"Go easy on the praise, Max," he said. "I'm not certain enough of Zelda's stability of character to expose her to superlatives or encourage her incipient egomania." (*To Doctor.*) Doctor, why did I marry him, anyway? (*Angrily.*) Of course I loved and married the artist in him! But I should've loved the artist in *myself*. And he should've, too. (*SHE finds another sheet of paper. Writing.*) Artist. (*Dropping the paper.*) The irony of it all is this — *I am his books.* (*To audience.*) Did you ever read his first book, "This Side of Paradise?" I ask everyone that, because a lot of people don't remember. But I do. My fairy tale began with its publication. And then there were gold-leaf kings and champagne sunshine and velvet nights. Francis-Francis-Scott-Scott-Fitzgerald-Fitzgerald. And me. Zelda Sayre. Miss Alabama Nobody. (*Curtsying.*) I was that little fish that swims about under the shark and lives indelicately on its refuse. That's the way it was. Life passed over me like a vast black shadow, and I swallowed with relish whatever it dropped. And I loved him. I loved Scott. Without him, everything was pale and pathetic. I trailed in the wake of his thoughts. I drowned in his image. Six, fiv— (*Pause.*) People, you see, relinquish the sacred fire with such reluctance, once they've possessed its scathing light. They seem to like the little blisters full of their own chemistry, and to grow fond of the scorching of their own skins. I've bored so many vistas through to unhappiness and collapsibility, I spend all my energy turning my eyes away. So, without complaint or remorse, I eat the stone. Six, five four. (*To Doctor.*) Say, Doc, did you ever work the Ouija board? You psychiatrists really ought to try it. You might have more success. I worked it once. The only answer I got was "dead, dead, dead." I got scared and quit. (*As Doctor.*) And now, Mrs. Fitzgerald, you will count down from three, and you will awaken relaxed, refreshed and rejuvenated. (*To Doctor.*) Three, two, one. So long, Doc.

(*SHE finds her reflection in the decanter on the desk.*)

ZELDA. (*To herself.*) "Rejuvenated" was perhaps a bit strong. (*To audience.*) The trouble is, I believed I was like the mythical salamander, able to live in fire and not be harmed. But I was harmed. And so was Scott. (*To Scott.*) I pray for you, Scott, and my prayer is communion with what is right. And what is right, my dear Goofo, is that you're dead and can no longer drive a steamroller over my pulverized ego. (*To the departed Doctor.*) You should've been here today, Doctor. But don't worry. I've brought you up to date. (*Picking up paper.*) Confident, exceptional, stable, artist ... (*Writing.*) Somebody. (*SHE picks up the lipstick and reads the label.*) Katie's

"Passion Poppy." (*SHE opens the tube of lipstick. Singing.*)
> We were two little babes in the wood
> Two little babes, oh, so good!

(*SHE applies the lipstick, looking at her image in the decanter.*)

> ZELDA. (*Singing.*)
> Two little hearts, two little heads,
> Longed to be home in their two little beds.

(*SHE takes one last look at the reflection of her bright red lips in the decanter.*)

> ZELDA. Hello, Zelda.

(*SHE contemptuously kicks at the knitting, which is lying on the floor.*)

> ZELDA. G'bye, Purl. (*During the following, SHE puts the lipstick back in the drawer and drops her sketch pad and pencil into the pillow case. Singing.*)
> So two little birds built a nest
> Where the two little babes went to rest,
> While the breeze, hov'ring nigh, sang a last
>   lullaby
> To the two little —

(*LOUDSPEAKER.*)

TAPED VOICE. (*As nurse.*) Your attention, patients. The dining room is now open. I repeat, the dining room is open.

ZELDA. (*Exiting with style.*) To hell with the dining room! Would somebody call me a cab?

(*Stage goes BLACK.*)

THE END

PROPERTY LIST

COSTUME:
Shapeless, plain dress, brown or gray
Baggy sweater
Ring
White jacket (Dr. Carroll's)

FURNITURE:
Desk
Desk chair
Desk lamp
Side chair
Traditional patient's couch
Coat tree
Bookcases
Floor lamp
Large rug

ACCESSORIES:
Striped pillow case
Drawing pencil in case
Sketch pad in case
Knitting with large needles in case
Cigarette/music box on desk
Cigarettes in box
Cigarette lighter
Ashtray on desk
Letter opener on desk
Telephone on desk
Writing pen on desk

Golfing trophies on bookcases
Drinking cup on desk
Chrome decanter on desk
Files full of papers in drawer
Lipstick in drawer
Books

About the Author

William Luce's Broadway and London success, THE BELLE OF AMHERST, starred actress Julie Harris and was directed by Charles Nelson Reilly. Miss Harris won her fifth Tony Award as Best Actress of 1977 for this portrayal of American poet Emily Dickinson. Luce adapted the play for an IBM Television Special, which received an Emmy nomination for Best Actress, and two Christopher Awards. The record album of the play received a Grammy Award. More recently, Thames Television in London aired a new production of THE BELLE OF AMHERST, starring actress Claire Bloom and directed by Adrian Brown. The production received the International Emmy Award for 1987.

Luce was a Writers Guild Award nominee for his CBS movie, THE LAST DAYS OF PATTON. It starred George C. Scott and Eva Marie Saint. The director was Delbert Mann. Luce also received a WGA nomination for his CBS movie, THE WOMAN HE LOVED, which starred Jane Seymour, Anthony Andrews, Olivia De Havilland and Julie Harris. Its director was Charles Jarrott. The movie received two Emmy nominations, as did the CBS movie, LUCY AND DESI: BEFORE THE LAUGHTER, co-authored by Luce and directed by Charles Jarrott.

Luce's play, BRONTË, was filmed in Ireland by Irish Television. Based on the life of Charlotte Brontë, it starred actress Julie Harris and was directed by Delbert Mann. Miss Harris also performed the play on WGBH's Masterpiece Radio Theatre. It was directed by Elinor Stout. This production won the Peabody Award, the Ohio State Award and Columbia University's Armstrong Award. Caedmon Records produced an album of the play. Miss Harris presented Luce's stage version of BRONTË in many theaters.

About the Author

Luce's play, LILLIAN, is based on the memoirs of playwright Lillian Hellman. LILLIAN premiered at The Cleveland Play House, then moved to Kennedy Center and Broadway. The play starred Tony-winning actress Zoe Caldwell, and was directed by Robert Whitehead.

Actress Piper Laurie performed Luce's play, THE LAST FLAPPER, in theaters across the country. The play is based on the life of Zelda Fitzgerald, wife of F. Scott Fitzgerald, and was directed by Charles Nelson Reilly. An earlier off-Broadway version of the play, titled ZELDA, starred actress Olga Bellin and was directed by Paul Roebling.

BRAVO, CARUSO! is Luce's play about the famed Italian tenor, Enrico Caruso. The play had its world premiere early in 1991 in celebration of the seventy-fifth anniversary of The Cleveland Play House. The play starred Joseph Mascolo and Joseph Sicari, and was directed by Peter Mark Schifter.

CPSIA information can be obtained at www.ICGtesting.com
Printed in the USA
LVOW05s2032150114

369568LV00019B/243/P